unrequited feelings

leslie b

unrequited feelings

ISBN: 9798857293867

chapters

overthinking

the riskiest thing
is to put all your love
into one singular person

where will you go
if one day they decide
they don't want you anymore?

you don't get to choose
if you get hurt in this world
but you do have a say
in who hurts you

- *i choose you*

i remember
that first night
we stayed up past 3am
and all we did was talk

i remember
thinking that i could
listen to you talk
forever
and how i've never felt that way
about anyone before

i remember
that night
at 3am
that was the moment
i fell in love

have you ever
loved someone
so much
that it scares you?

i'm thinking you are someone i could really like, and that scares the hell out of me. being with you is so easy. it's like we understand each other completely, and that's something i struggle to find with everyone else. but i'm scared. because i think i am the kind of person that throws myself completely when i love something. i've spent a long time trying to get here to where i am today. i honestly don't know if i can do it all over again. i know this is all a lot, and i shouldn't put it on you. it's not fair. but it is how i truly feel. i don't know how to love halfway. i throw myself into it completely and it ruins me every single time. i overthink the things i care about and i predict things before it happens, and sometimes it doesn't happen the way i predict so it's really my overthinking that ruins it. i don't know how to change that. i'm sensitive to the things i care about and i need you to be okay with that. i need assurance, but i will never ask for it. you make me want to throw myself completely into you and i know the spark we create could light up the whole world. but i'm terrified that one day you will stop reciprocating and i will keep lighting myself on fire to attract you and you won't reciprocate and i will burn and i will burn and i will burn and that scares the fuck out of me.

- a letter i will never send

hope is a dangerous thing
for some things you see coming
but you let it come
and fuck you up anyway

there was this
unspoken silence
between us

it was like
we both wanted it
but neither of us knew
how to begin

i never knew what i wanted
until i met you

- *i wish you wanted me back too*

i remember it was
on the third day of the new year
5am or something,
you were soundly asleep
breathing rhythmically
like you were focusing on a dream

i moved over and put my arms around you
i wanted to give you some warmth,
i remember it lingered for a minute
and you pushed my arm away
still half-asleep,
that was the first time you ever reacted that way

about half an hour later,
5:49am
i remember because i got up for a cup of water
you were still soundly asleep
i rested my hands on your thighs
it was subtle,
i just wanted to touch you
have a connecting point to your skin
while we dozed

i remember it lingered for a little while
and you moved your body away
it was subtle,
but your intention lingered
and that lingering feeling started to eat at my chest
how could something so subtle have such a big
hurt?

i don't know if it was silly
that i had an intuition that night
or silly that my intuition turned out to be right
but somehow that night
i knew that this
was a beginning to an end

i mean it when i say that i'm very sensitive to
other people's energies. i can sense when
something is off, usually as it happens. sometimes
people say that i am over-reading, but most of the
time they just haven't processed it themselves yet.
i feel like emotionally, every person i've ever
liked has left me before i left them. but physically,
it always seems like i can't stay put. but the truth
is, i just don't want to be around someone that i
can slowly feel doesn't want me to be around
them anymore.

is it a curse or a blessing
for someone to be able to
feel all of these feelings
so deeply?

it's just one of those nights
where i'm checking my phone
picking it up
putting it down
picking it up again
opening our conversation
even though there are
no new notifications

- just wanted to make sure

the less attention you gave me
the more i craved for it

waiting an hour
to get a text back
a one word reply
dry
like you're not interested at all,
texting back in the next minute
waiting an hour
to get a next text back

- *a cycle that hurts*

are you busy
or are you with
someone else?

- *overthinking*

maybe you're busy
and i am just freaking out
at your lack of response
or interest, even
or maybe i am just unnecessarily
clingy
needy
emotional,
maybe there is nothing wrong
and i am just overthinking
but missing someone
who doesn't miss you back
hurts
but it's fine,
i know i will just be
overthinking myself to sleep
tonight

8 billion people
in this world
and i can't stop thinking
about one

i can't read your mind
and you can't read mine

i wonder
if things will be different
if we said to each other
what we truly think

i know you're too busy
to miss me
and i am sitting here
wondering all the what if's

if this is love, it shouldn't be this difficult.

communication shouldn't be so hard. you shouldn't have to second guess everything you have in mind. you shouldn't have to apologize all the time. you shouldn't have to constantly feel like you're not enough. or that the next moment you are suddenly too much. you shouldn't have to keep telling yourself that you need to be more understanding and to keep trying and trying and never have it being enough. you shouldn't have to feel like you're backed into a corner and everything you do seems to be wrong despite how desperately you want to make it work.

if this is love, it shouldn't hurt this bad.

there shouldn't be this deep ache in your heart where you are constantly finding yourself gasping for air. you shouldn't have to feel like you are going to hurl yourself inside out despite barely eating for 3 days. you shouldn't be finding yourself wide-eyed awake at 3am having a million things running in your mind when your eyelids desperately want to shut but your mind won't shut up. you shouldn't be running around in circles trying to pinpoint the downfall of it all but never really knowing the answer, trying to tell yourself that it doesn't matter, but the cycle torments you over and over and over again.

if this is love, you shouldn't have to beg for it.

you shouldn't be finding yourself on your knees alone in your room whispering "please, please, please" a million times. you were never a religious person, but there you were at 4:17am praying to every god you know - saying that this is the one, this is the one. if you had 3 wishes, you would spend all 3 of them wishing that they would stay.

if this is love, you shouldn't be this sad.

you have never really wanted anything, but you want this so badly. you want them to be the one, so so much. your heart is breaking and your mind won't stop racing. everything you do leads back to the same person. every thought leads back to the same person. deep down you feel like this probably wouldn't work out anymore, your wishes never come true anyway. but you want it to. but you want it to.

i don't know
how long i can keep doing
this little dance with you

pretending to be casual
when you are all
i can think about

in the last 10 mins
i checked my phone 10 times
3 of them wasn't you
7 was just my imagination

i spent 20 mins
deciding
when is the best time
to text you back

i wonder
if you are busy
or are you playing
the same game back?

if you want me too much,
i will not want you back.
if you want me too little,
i will move on.

- *a little game*

you've destroyed me
by being
so far away

you never know
how strong your love is
until you have to start
loving them from a distance

i don't know
how many times
i can keep doing this
but it *hurts*
to love someone
who doesn't love you back

when i'm alone
i want to be able to feel,
when i'm with someone
i just want it to stop hurting

- *a contradiction*

thoughts can't seem to stop
pouring out of me tonight
my heart hurts
but no one seems to care
all this pain inside me
but i have no solution
are they really the problem
if they have no idea
that they were the problem?

i can't read your mind
and i can't keep filling my mind
with another scenario
to overthink about

i don't know what i want anymore
i thought i wanted you
but tonight i'm not so sure anymore
all these things you said to me
i'm not sure what to believe anymore
the only thing i'm thinking right now is
i don't know how long i can do this anymore

how do you fix something
if you don't know
what is broken?

my brain is in a mess tonight
you are still here
but my heart is already aching
i can't stop asking myself
how long more before you go?
i know deep down
i don't have you anymore
and i am not okay with it
there's a million things
i want to say to you
but i don't know where to begin
i have a feeling
whatever i say
will end up to be wrong
and i will just push you further away
i wish i could read your mind
but i think i already know
what your answer is

i can feel this coming to an end
but i don't want it to end

unrequited feelings

it makes me sad
because i feel like
we barely started
and now we are already
falling apart

we could have
created a spark
that would ignite the world
but you were too afraid
to commit

i miss you
a lot,
but lately it seems like
it doesn't matter
anymore

the lack of desire
you have for me
when i'm around you
hurts

i only told myself
what i wanted to hear
and i overlooked the things
happening in front of me

i focused too much
on what you said in the past
and too little
on what you are saying now

you've made those promises
i wanted to believe
you wouldn't lie to me
but people change
and sometimes
they change their mind
about you

got my own hopes up
because
i desperately wanted it to work
and that was the beginning
of me
breaking my own heart

the more i love you
the more it hurts

- i don't think that's how it should work

i was alone
and all i wanted
was to be able to feel
something
anything,

and then i found you
and i was happy for awhile
until i wasn't
until it started to hurt
and all i could think of
was that i don't want to feel
anything
anymore

- *a cynical cycle*

we promised
to light up the world together
but you stood there and watched
as i lit myself on fire

today i miss you like hell. i woke up 3 hours earlier than i usually do and the first thing i think of is you. i checked my phone and you haven't responded to my text from 8pm last night. i wonder what you were doing and who you were with. the message wasn't even about anything. i try to focus on the one thing that actually matters in this moment - going back to sleep. but i can't do it anymore. i've been awake for too long and my thoughts are now spiraling. what happened between us? where did we went wrong? how do we go back to how it was before? is that even possible? i checked my phone again. obviously nothing has happened in the 20 seconds since i last picked it up. i don't even know what i was expecting. all i know is that i recognize this sinking feeling in my chest. i know what is coming. oh yeah. it is going to hurt.

the answer lies
in all the things
we did not say
to each other

i'm not sure if there's anything
more painful
than feeling the person
you gave your heart to
slowly losing interest in you
and you can feel
the love in your heart
drying out

was it my fault
for giving you a chance
or was it your fault
for breaking your promise?

- *does it matter?*

letting you go
feels like losing a part of me
the newfound love i had for myself
when i first met you

but things are not the same
as it used to be
and the love i had for myself
is now replaced with hurt and disappointment
mixed with a tinge of hope,
perhaps things could go back to
how it was before

it's not over but it already is
deep down i think we both know it
the present will never be the past
but we keep trying to find our way
back to what it once was

i'm sorry that i keep doing this to myself
i don't think i am ready to let go yet
but then again,
when are we ever truly ready?

the ending has been written
but i am not ready to face it yet
i know the fear is mostly irrational
give me a little more time
i will find my way there

we had everything we wanted
but you wanted more

there was something
unspoken
about the way you left
i knew
something was off
but i didn't ask
i didn't know
it was going to be
the last time
i'll ever see you

your hesitation
gave me the answers
i needed

i knew
this was going to happen

i could tell
from the difference in response
the way you looked at me
the lack of details
when you tell me something

i knew
something has changed
but i didn't want to
confirm my suspicions

maybe i'm just overthinking
and maybe there isn't a problem
and there might be
if i raise up a non-existential issue

a few days later,
it happened
you said everything i was thinking
and it has never hurt so much
to be right

you gave up on us
before it even begin

are you fucking kidding me
was my first reaction
when you sent me that text
telling me it was over

i read through your justifications
the things you wrote
to make yourself feel better
and no i do not forgive you
for telling me
truths you should have told me
at least a month earlier
there's someone else
why am i only finding out about this now
you waited
until the last moment
until you were absolutely certain
before you dropped me

thanks for hurting me
when you absolutely
didn't have to

i could tell you
all about what i'm thinking
but why would it matter?
what does it change?
you've made up your mind
and the only thing i can do
is to accept it

i've said too much
to you
and still,
it wasn't enough

you fed fire to my soul
and i burned
with passion for you
then you went ahead
and left me unattended
so now i just burn
in agony

why did you say yes
to something
you knew
you didn't want?

it is the most painful feeling
watching the person you love
choose someone else
over you

at what point
did you decide
that you don't want me
anymore?

- i can't stop thinking about this

you can't
treat people like shit
and expect them to
not get mad over it

if words could kill
i would have died,
a thousand times over

after everything
we've been through
i was not expecting it
to end this way

it was in your eyes
that i knew
you were in love with me
and it was in your eyes
when i realized
you no longer love me

- *same eyes, different story*

i had all these things
i wanted to tell you
i don't think it matters
anymore

you had me and you decided that
you didn't want it

it is time
i learn to let go
if you wanted to, you would
i've said enough
for you to know how i feel
i can't keep waiting
for an answer
that isn't going to come

today
i say goodbye to you
i close my eyes
and i wait for the hurt
to come

rock-bottom

how many more times
can i be broken
i can't keep putting myself
back together

it might be the
worst feeling in the world
when the person
who wanted you
changes their mind

leaving is easy
you just walk away
and never look back

it is what comes after
that they don't tell you about

- *what's next?*

after you left
the smell of you
continues to
linger

the first few days are the hardest
you wake up in the middle of the night
the breakup replaying in your mind
what did i do wrong?
you rethink every scenario that happened
how it felt so right
at one moment in time
maybe i should have said that
you tried to look for the moment
when things started going bad
maybe it was something you said
or a specific thing you did
or didn't do,
that started the turbulence
and led to this moment
every time you close your eyes
you can feel where it hurts
it's over
but it doesn't feel like it
it will take you awhile more
of replaying everything that happened
for you to finally realize
that this
was never your fault

i really really wanted us to work out.

you said
you don't have to explain to me
i get it
but i don't think
you ever did

it wasn't you
that hurt me the most
it was the expectations
i've built for myself
because i believed you
and now i am suffering
the consequences
of my own beliefs

i don't know how to find the balance between wanting to love someone and not wanting to get hurt.

i only had myself
to blame
for getting hurt
in the end

it was in your presence
that i found
my sense of belonging
it didn't matter
what i was doing
you were always
right next to me
now that you're gone
nothing feels right
without you
i don't know where to go
anymore

it's hard being the person who falls first.

someone once said to me

if you want something
very badly
set it free
if it comes back to you
it's yours forever

if it doesn't
it was never yours
to begin with

- i really wish you came back

how many times
can you miss a person
until it doesn't hurt
anymore?

i think we were too obsessed with wanting it to
work out that we forgot to enjoy what we had.

it's mad
how you can love someone
and not be happy
and not even realize it

you looked me in the eyes
and told me
you are the only one
i heard the conviction in your voice
and never doubted you
for a second

i guess what happened was
you changed your mind halfway
and it never came up
so you conveniently
forgot
to tell me

technically
you didn't lie
but it still makes you
a liar

was it my fault
for believing you
when you said the things
you did?

i remember
how much you mattered to me
and how quickly
you stopped mattering

would it have
worked out between us
if there wasn't someone else?

- *questions i ask the universe*

you never said sorry to me
how can one person
be so cruel
and not see it?

it's hard to believe
the good in people
after people like you

some days
i really wish
we have never met

i wish i've never
responded to that DM you sent
never said hi back
never stayed up till 3am
texting you back
on the first day

i wish you never broke my heart
i wish you never met someone else
i wish you were honest enough to tell me
i wish you never made me feel like i was happy
when my entire world was crashing
and i couldn't see it
i didn't know

i wish i could take back
all i've given to you
but it's too late now
you've given me a glimpse
of what it means to be happy
and i wish
i wouldn't keep thinking about you
even after all of this

i wish things were different
but i'll never know

too many feelings
for too many people
i haven't had the courage
to put it into words

we were never
just friends
and we can never go back
to being friends

unrequited feelings

at one point we were everything
now i can't even speak your name

- *nothing lasts forever*

after you,
i don't know
how to trust anyone
anymore

you let me down
i hope you know that
i know you know that
you broke my heart
someone
who has been nothing
but genuine to you
from day one
i know you probably regret it
but it won't take away
all the hurt
you've given to me
and no
i won't forgive you
but i will allow myself
to forget about you

i can still feel
the exact part of my chest
where it hurts

- *heartbreak is a physical feeling*

i want you to know
how much
i was hurt by you

but i know
the best way to move on
is to not think about it anymore

we are all really
just trying to find love
but somehow
we keep getting hurt
in the process

- *hopeless romantics*

before i let you go
i want you to know this
you were everything to me
at one point in time

i thought you were the one
at the beginning
i don't know which point
i stopped believing

before i let you go
i hope you know
that i've tried my best
to make this work

you can't force compatibility
and i know
i will not be happy with you
anymore

it's over
but i will still
think of you
forever

moving on

i don't know how else to move on
other than to keep thinking about you
i'll take in all the pain
and let it hurt
until i'm used to it
until it doesn't bother me as much
until the hurt starts to fade
until one day
i might not notice it anymore

- i don't know how else to do it

you will hurt
a lot
and you will be okay
again

the people we love
they become part of us
we carry their memories
and we see flashes of them
from other people we meet

and i will carry your memory
for the rest of eternity

what is coming
is better than what is gone
i have a hard time believing
that i will ever find someone
better than you

trust is something
i'm trying to be better at
i know it's going to be
a lonely road ahead
and i can only pray that
i make it all the way through

it's been months
since we last talked
things have sort of fizzled
i wonder if there is anything left
anymore

i guess it doesn't matter
if i'm choosing to move on
i wish more people would tell you
that leaving an unhappy situation
doesn't make you happy
it leaves you lonely
and that's another feeling
they don't tell you too much about

you will be sad
for awhile
and you will be
okay

the truth is
i was fine before you
and i know i will be fine
after you,
although it sure doesn't feel like it
right now,
but i know it will be fine
i will be fine
i will be fine

you've been through this before
you can do this again

i used to be happy
when i see your name
on my stories

now i question daily
how long should it be
before i block you

it's crazy
how quickly
people can stop
to matter

you can't keep waiting
for a message
that isn't going to come

some day
you will meet someone
and all of this pain
you're going through right now
will be worth it

one of the hardest lessons
i had to learn was
you can't love someone
into loving you back
i gave you everything i had
but you didn't care
it wasn't what i gave
it was what you wanted
and the truth is
no matter how much
you want someone
it won't work
if they don't want you back

you did not
do anything wrong
it just didn't work out
that's all

- note to self

the more i looked at your profile
the less it hurts
it's like i can almost see myself
slowly losing interest
in you

if i can't have
all of you
then i don't want
any of you

most nights
i wish that things could
go back to how it was
before

some nights
i know that deep down,
i don't want that

you deserve someone
who is willing to stay for you

things don't always
work out the way
you want it to
and i am trying
to be okay with that

i think
when this is over
i will finally
be able to
breathe

sometimes i catch myself
wondering
how you are doing now
and i realized
i don't care anymore

if you can't be loyal,
nothing else matters

i kept trying to
find someone
to complete me

turns out
the person i was looking for
was me all along

perhaps
the best thing to do
is to truly not give a fuck
about anything
or anyone
at all

today
is the first day
i saw 11:11
and didn't think of you

it takes a lot of power
to not cascade myself down
into this darkness

- *self control*

you breaking my heart
was probably the best thing
that happened to me

you showed me
the people i need to avoid
and you taught my heart
how much more it could take
despite being completely broken

i was a sadder person
because of you
but i am also a stronger person
because of you

after you
it's not going to be easy
for anyone
to hurt me again

meeting
you
changed
everything

you don't need someone
to complete you
you have yourself
and that is all you need

if i ever saw you
on the streets again
i will simply
keep walking

i was cleaning my room today
and i found an old picture of us
oh god
i don't remember
the last time i thought of you

on the picture
i looked happy
and i think i really was
but i don't remember that feeling anymore
honestly,
i don't even think i recognized myself

it was today that i thought of you again
and i miss you.
but i miss the old version of you
the one that doesn't exist anymore
and i'm not the same person
i used to be either

memories
they have a special way
of doing things to you
it's been six months
since i last thought of you
i loved what we had
and i am glad
that it is over

i've wrote about you so much that at this point you just kind of feel like a fictional character to me.

the way you left
made me glad that
it didn't work out
between us

i don't need you anymore.

writing is the only way i know how to feel better.

things don't always happen the way you want them to. and when it doesn't, it hurts.

i've spent too many nights overthinking myself to sleep. waking up too early feeling like i can't breathe because my mind won't stop racing. i never knew what to do with myself, until i found writing. it's the only thing that makes me feel at peace.

i wrote "getting over you" after one of the most hurtful experiences in my life. i did not expect so many people to find resonance in my words. thank you for validating my feelings. and thank you for making me feel like i wasn't the only one in the world going through this hurt.

my second book "unrequited feelings" is based off a recent experience i had of liking someone who changed their mind about you. it's a horrible feeling. but i felt more empowered this time to handle it because i knew there are people out there who feel the same way as i do.

if you're going through something similar, all i can tell you is that you are not alone. i can't make it better, but i am here with you. and i love you.

thank you for saving my life.

leslie

Also by Leslie B,

getting over you

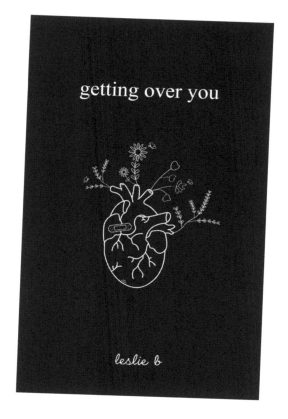

Available on Amazon

Made in the USA
Middletown, DE
08 September 2024